THE BOY WHO MET JESUS
and A MESSAGE FOR HUMANITY

by IMMACULEE ILIBAGIZA

www.immaculee.com

The Boy Who Met Jesus and A Message for Humanity

First Printing: July 2016
Copyright 2016 by Immaculee Ilibagiza
ISBN: 978-0-9850548-8-5
Library of Congress Control Number: 2016910436

Printed by:
Immaculee LLC
lefttotell@ymail.com
www.immaculee.com

Published in the United States of America
Edited by Judith Weible
Type and cover by Janice Stallings

OTHER BOOKS BY IMMACULEE ILIBAGIZA

Immaculee Ilibagiza's books are also in electronic format.

Dedicated to you My Lord for loving us so much to come to us. To all who will carry the torch, and share this message.
May God bless you and reward your efforts.

CONTENTS

It should be no surprise that God would speak to us, His creation, through a series of ul-tra-powerful messages given to a randomly cho-sen little boy. After all, it has happened before. The Biblical story of a young Israelite boy named David, who would later become king of Israel, comes to mind.

However, for our Creator to choose not just a little boy, but a *pagan* little boy to deliver spe-cial soul-saving messages to the people of the world—one who did not know Jesus, had never read a word of Holy Scripture nor set foot inside a church? This act by our loving God is not only a surprise but also a puzzling one at that.

Segatashya's story of meeting Jesus and then receiving and delivering the special messages He gave him are meant to give all of us an overwhelming desire to follow God and achieve Heaven. Isn't that our goal as children of God? Well, through these messages, we have a straightforward, unequivocal way to achieve that goal.

The words from our Savior to Segatashya are far beyond extraordinary; they give us all we need to know. The next step is to accept them and then to live them by putting them into practice in our everyday lives.

We are indebted to Immaculee for bringing the treasured messages of Jesus to this little pagan boy through this special book. She was blessed to have met Segatashya in person before his martyred death during the horrendous genocide that ravaged the African country of Rwanda in 1994. When they met Segatashya was no longer a pagan; he was Jesus' special little messenger.

While Immaculee has written about Segatashya in her earlier writings, some of the messages contained here have never before been revealed. They are messages meant for this time when the world seems afire with rejection of God and His Son's sacrifice on the cross. It is yet another grace given to us to assist us in reaching eternal life.

—*Wayne Weible*

Many of you know me from my previous books, or maybe through my retreats, speeches or pilgrimages. Perhaps this is the first time you are reading my work. Whoever you are, you are my brother or my sister. I wish you well on this journey and I am glad we are getting to take it together, I pray for you and please pray for me.

I couldn't wait any longer to write this book and share these messages with you. I wrote about this story extensively in my book titled, "*The Boy Who Met Jesus*". However, having written that book, I still find myself wanting a book that contains just the messages of Jesus through Segatashya. This is a book I want to keep in my purse, so I can read and reread or simply hand over to a friend without them getting caught up in the background stories.

These are messages you will want to memorize, practice everywhere you go and share whenever you can. Although I feel like every book I have written is the most important, I know for sure that these are the most vital messages I can share with you. These are messages given by Our Lord, Jesus Christ. It doesn't get any better or any more meaningful than that. These messages will answer many of your questions about life: how the end of the world will unfold and what will happen on the Day of Judgment. They are messages that concern every human being!

I met Segatashya in person before he was killed during the genocide in Rwanda in 1994, a genocide that took more than a million innocent people. After reading so much about Segatashya's interactions with Jesus, I was so fortunate to meet him personally and have a conversation with him about his apparitions. It meant so much to me to hear his story first hand. That is why I will simply introduce him and let him tell you his story; you will read it as if he is talking to you. This book does not include every message Segatashya received from Jesus, but it includes the main message he shared when he went to speak in public, the message he himself considered the core message. Jesus told Segetashya that this message had to reach the world so Segetashya traveled to neighboring countries, such as Congo and Burundi, to share this same message.

The story of Segatashya was preceded by an important event in Rwanda. In 1981 in a place called Kibeho, something supernatural occurred, something unlike anything ever experienced in our country. On November 28, a teenage girl in high school named Alphonsine Mumureke shocked the world by saying that she saw the Virgin Mary, Mother of God, with her own eyes, and she spoke to her. She was attending a boarding school, run by nuns with only 120 students. To the astonishment of everyone Mary continued to appear to Alphonsine, despite how heavily the other students persecuted her. Many resented her newfound popularity so she begged Mary to show herself to other students who were not her friends so people would believe her.

Alphonsine said that Mary was giving her a message that concerned everyone, but many thought she was going crazy. Later two more students, totally unrelated to Alphonsine, claimed to see Mary. The most pious was Anatalie Mukamazimpaka as well as Alphonsine's harshest critic, Marie Claire Mukangango. After this happened, the other students were convinced that the apparitions were not made up. It became big news, not only in the village of Kibeho, but also in the whole country. These apparitions attracted hundreds of thousands of people, from all over the world. Radio, TV and print news media came to share the supernatural news. No one could ignore what was happening. The main message Mary gave was a reminder to the world about what her Son Jesus had told us... to love one another, to forgive one another.

The girls were told the hour and date Mary would come to see them next, and the news traveled throughout the country very quickly. By the time Mary appeared to them, there were thousands of people waiting, believers and nonbelievers.

A podium was built for the visionaries to stand on while they conversed with Mary. From the moment Mary appeared, the children said they felt like they had entered into another world that was more beautiful and more peaceful. Mary's visits were not rushed, she spent up to eight hours talking with them, and during this time the girls couldn't feel anything from the outside world. Medical doctors and psychiatrics examined each girl to be certain she wasn't suffering from mental illness. They injected needles into their bodies, they burned them with fire and they couldn't feel anything while they were talking to Mary. The messages they shared were studied extensively by the Church to make sure they were from Heaven and not from hell. My family was among the spectators and it changed our lives.

On July 2, 1982, we were surprised to hear that there was another visionary, this time it was a boy. The boy passed all the tests just as the girls had done. His name was Segatashya and he was a pagan, who had never been in school or in church. He was a shepherd from a poor family who lived to support his family.

Segatashya didn't see Mary at first like the other visionaries, but he saw Jesus himself. The first time it happened, he was resting under a tree after going to check on his parent's bean field. All of a sudden a voice spoke to Segatashya telling him he wanted to give him a message to share with everyone. Segatashya was 14 years old at the time, so, as you can imagine, he was reluctant at first, as he will tell you himself.

After that initial meeting, Jesus visited Segatashya many more times and gave him messages to share with everyone. Jesus taught him prayers and how to pray to God, he even chose a name for him for his baptism, the name Emmanuel, just like Jesus. He taught him the rosary, catechism, and all about the bible, asking him to read it and to go to church. The meetings of Jesus and Segatashya happened in public, in the presence of thousands of people just as Mary did with the girls, Jesus would give him the date and time he would come to visit him, and He always came exactly on time. They spoke in Segatashya's native language, Kinyarwanda, and the apparitions lasted many hours.

The theologians asked Segatashya many difficult questions. If he didn't know the answer, he would tell them that he would ask Jesus, and later they were surprised by his intelligent answers. Segatashya was also privileged to see Mary, the Mother of Jesus. I will never forget when he shared about the first time he saw Mary; he said Jesus told him that He wanted to introduce him to somebody special. Segatashya said Jesus had a special joy in his face. Then Mary came from the right side of Jesus as if she had been standing behind him. Segatashya said he would never forget the beauty he saw in her face, in her whole being. Our Lord told him then, "*This is my mother, I want you to love her as you love yourself, and I want you to respect her as you respect me*". Later he was asked to compare their beauty, he said, "*Jesus is a man, a very good looking man, he is God, you can see it, you can feel it, He is merciful, you can see it, but the beauty of His mother, I am unable to describe it, she is like a dove, beyond words*".

I find myself, in prayer, trying to imagine how Mary, my favorite saint, looks and even though I have not seen her. I can still feel chills on my skin, a joy and peace I can't describe just imagining the love and beauty of the Mother of God and my mother.

Jesus and Mary both gave Segatashya a message to share with the world. Sometimes they would ask Segatashya and the other visionaries at Kibeho to repeat what they had said to all who were watching the apparitions. Many times, they asked us, the crowd; to help them spread their messages; to help them reach their children around the world.

I am writing this book to answer that call. I hope you like it; I hope it lights your way and I hope you will carry the torch and reach Jesus' other children and share with those you can. I pray that we will meet, if not here, in heaven to live happily for eternity.

—Immaculee

JESUS FIRST SPEAKS TO SEGATASHYA

My name is Segatashya. I am one of the children of Kibeho who was extremely blessed to see
Jesus and Mary. I was a shepherd at the time and
took care of my father's animals. However, on the
day I saw Jesus for the first time, I was not keep-
ing the flock. On that day, my parents had sent
me 20 minutes away from our home to check on
our bean field to see if the crop was ready to be
picked. When I arrived, I could not see the beans
clearly. This will sound strange, but they looked

1

shiny and beautiful. I had never seen beans that looked like that. I thought I was seeing things because I was tired after spending so much time in the sun. I asked a man nearby if he could look with me and tell me if he thought the beans were ripe. He said, "*They are alright child, can't you see?*"

Then I felt an overwhelming tiredness and went to sit in the shade, under a tree near the road. I heard a voice that called me by my name, **"Segatashya".** That was my only name as I had not been baptized. Neither my parents, nor myself, had ever attended a church or a school. The voice called a second time, **"You there, my child".** I looked around to see who was calling me and from where the voice was coming. I could see no one. Then the voice called to me for the third time, and I felt an urgency to answer, so I replied, "*Yes.*"

The voice said, *"You there, child, if you were given a message to deliver to the world, would you deliver it?"*

At first I was afraid of this person who wanted to give me a message for the world, but at the same time, I felt joy in my heart and answered, *"Yes I will do what you ask, but who are you? If people ask who sent me, what am I going to tell them?"*

The voice, which was Jesus, said, *"You know how men are, if I tell you my name, there may be no one who will listen to you. I hear them say that if anyone comes in the name of Jesus Christ, do not trust them. You see, they might not understand or believe you if you reveal my identity."*

I told him, *"If you are truly Jesus Christ, they will believe you, as long as you are willing to help them to believe. For me, I will do my best, providing you give me the gift of wisdom when I am speaking the words of your message."*

Then the voice said, *"I am Jesus Christ. For you to prove to me that you will really be capable of giving my message to people in the future, I want you to go right now and give this message to those who are working in the house of a certain Mr. Hubert. Tell them this message in these words."*

"Jesus Christ sent me here today to tell you, and all men to renew your hearts. The day is coming when things will really get hard for humanity. You must change your heart while there is still time. Soon those who have refused to repent will not be able to do so. Let those who know that I set foot on earth, know that I am on my way back to take those who have worked well for Me to heaven for their eternal reward."

So I went to tell the people who were working in the house what I had been told. As I was speaking to them, and without me realizing, my clothes came off, and I was naked. Then a lady who was there wrapped me in her clothes and said, *"Child, you are naked, whom do you think will listen to you in that condition?"*

I asked the voice, *"Why did you make me naked?"*

Jesus told me to tell them, ***"The Son of Man came into the world a long time ago, before you existed, and they stripped Him naked. Do you think that He didn't reach heaven just because He was naked? Know that He is the one who has just performed this miracle now. This is a sign that will not remain eternally but that will be remembered forever."***

Then Jesus told me, ***"Thank you, this is enough for today, now turn your face up and look at the one who has been talking to you and look at Me well."***

I looked up and felt like I had disappeared into another world; a world more beautiful than the one I was in and a world without inhabitants. It was totally new and different. I was all alone, standing in a vast sea of vibrant, sweet-smelling, green grass. Then, suddenly, in a brilliant white light, appeared the most handsome man I had ever seen floating high above me. He was standing in the middle of some beautiful, white flowers. He looked like He was in His early 30s; He was of a dark-skinned complexion, neither black like the natives of Rwanda nor white like the Europeans or the church statues. He looked like a strong Rwandan man. He was dressed all in white clothes, and was wearing the traditional tunic of a Rwandan man. He wore a white robe and white clothes crossing his shoulders. He looked like the sun was shining from Him. In His presence, I felt total peace.

All the time He spoke to me in my native language: Kinyarwanda. And then He told me, *"Did you contemplate Me well?"*

I said, *"Yes Lord."*

Then He said, *"You did very well today my child, and you did very good delivering My message to these men. Now go and put into practice what I have told you to say, because it concerns you as well. If you continue to do well, I will see you next time, very soon."*

This was July 2, 1982. It was the beginning. I was 14 years old and the first born in my family. I was a pagan and had never gone to school or church. My parents and brothers had never been to school either (before the apparition). Neither had we the opportunity to go to church. The following year, I kept seeing Jesus in public, and He said goodbye to me in public on July 2, 1983, but He continued to appear to me in private.

PRAYER JOURNAL

PRAYER JOURNAL

SEGATASHYA QUESTIONS JESUS

———

Before I learned anything about Christianity, I asked many questions of Jesus, *"I hear people talking about God in different ways, different names. In Rwanda, they call Him Imana. In Congo, they commonly call Him Mungu. I hear them talking about the Virgin Mary, Jesus, Judas, Satan and more. Who do we have to love and respect among those?"*

Jesus said, ***"Whatever you do my child, do not love or respect Judas or Satan."***

I asked again, *"Among the rest, who should I love?"*

Jesus said, **"Of all the others you mentioned, if you love any of them sincerely with your heart, you have succeeded in fulfilling my messages of cleansing your heart for my return. Calling upon one name among the ones you mentioned will lead you to another, and all of them will lead you to love and truth. And anytime you find yourself in need, you may call upon any of those names and they will bring you what you need. My Blessed Mother will lead you to Me, and to the Father, and to the Holy Spirit, for we are one, we are not many."**

I responded to Jesus by saying, *"Thank you, I understand. But if I was really in trouble and needed help in a big hurry, which one of you up there in heaven has the most power and could help me out the quickest?"*

Jesus replied, *"Oh my child! What questions you dare to ask me!"*

I said, *"I don't mean to be disrespectful, Lord. But there is something I really need to know. You give me all these messages to pass along to people about repenting and the end of the world, and then everyone thinks I am crazy and wants to beat me up. They have damaged my parents' home and threaten my whole family. They have insulted my poor, defenseless mother. Even my mom and my dad have started calling me stupid for bringing all this trouble into their lives, especially when I can't provide them with simple answers to their questions. They call me a liar and are mean to me. Jesus, I wish you could tell me who the top person in heaven is, so I can get help fast, or else send down some bodyguards to provide me with security all the time. I suppose I would be better able to take care of myself if you gave me the same powers you had when you were on earth working miracles.*

I would have the whole truth in order to answer the questions myself without coming back to ask you all the time. So, why don't you give me all your power and your knowledge so I can properly defend myself?"

Jesus responded, **"Child, do you really think that if I gave you My power, and all the truth, you will use it in the right way?"**

I said, *"Well probably not. But I only ask because if I keep doing what you ask of me and go around preaching about the end of the world, someone might kill me just to shut me up. And then all of these messages you gave me would be useless because I would end up dying as you did."*

Then Jesus said to me, **"Are you willing to die for mankind?"**

I said, *"Well, it wouldn't be easy. I mean, no one wants to die for nothing."*

Jesus said, *"Who died for nothing? Child, I see that you are smiling and happy, but are you saying that I died for nothing?"*

I said, *"No Lord, forgive me. I sometimes get carried away when I am with you. I know you died for our sins, to save us because you love us. Thank you for your love and for all the answers you have given me, Lord. I will sing your praises and spread your messages all around the world with joy in my heart.*

Another time I asked Jesus, *"God knows everything - the past and the future. Did God create some people to go to heaven and others to go to hell?"*

Jesus said, *"God does not order people to go to hell. People choose to go to hell, or to go to heaven, because He gave each one free will. Each is given the independence to choose what they want."*

Jesus told me that Satan was the first child of God to disrespect Him and the first to sin against Him greatly.

He then explained to me what happened to Satan. *"Satan refused to listen to God. He left the rest of God's children and set himself aside from everyone in heaven. To this day, he does not yet have the heart to come back and apologize. You know sometimes, parents beg a child to be good and the child completely refuses. That is how Satan acted toward God. God remained with those who obeyed Him and want to obey Him. All that happened before the earth was created, and then Satan felt his loneliness but still refused to listen to God. Then he started to lie to other children God loves, so that they could be like him, and suffer like him because he doesn't love anyone. He just wanted them to be cursed like him, to suffer the same way and to offend God always by lying to His children whom He loves."*

Then I asked, *"Jesus you tell us to love our enemies, even when our enemies seem to be evil, sinful,* and harm us and to pray for those who persecute us, but didn't God fight a war against Satan and cast him into hell? You tell us that Satan is our greatest enemy and that we must fight against him and against his temptations. Will you please explain how, on the other hand, it seems obvious that you hate Satan and you are not forgiving him?"

Jesus said, **"Child, I do not hate Satan. On the contrary, it is Satan who hates me. If Satan would repent and sincerely ask for God to forgive his sins, then Satan would be forgiven and he would be allowed back in heaven. But for that to happen, Satan must repent sincerely from his heart. Now you answer this question for me, my child: do you know how many types of confessions there are?"**

I answered: "Yes, Lord, as you taught me, there are two ways for us to confess. The first way is by confessing our sins openly and being deeply sorrowful for having offended you. We must regret our wrongdoing *with all our hearts, sincerely ask for your forgiveness, and meaningfully commit ourselves to never repeat those sins again. The second way is by confessing our sins without being sorry and regretful in our hearts for having committed the sins and for having offended you. When we confess this way, we know that our repentance is only for show, to make ourselves look better in the eyes of others...and within our hearts we know that we will sin again as soon as we are able to."*

Jesus said, ***"Very well said, child! I am happy that you remember our lesson about what it is to confess truly from your heart. Now, can you understand what I mean when I say that Satan can only be forgiven if he confesses from the heart?"***

I said, *"Yes, Lord, I understand. But because Satan is the Great Liar, it will be difficult for him to ever confess from the heart. But I have much more to ask about this, Lord. I am sorry I have many ques-*

tions, but I need answers and you are not always clear, so please don't hide anything from me and speak plainly. When you send me to give people your messages they have questions too, so I must be able to answer them."

I have another question, *"You are telling me that I need to pass the message along to people and that they must repent because the state of the world is bad...because mankind has become so sinful the world is now on the edge of ruin. But then, you also tell me, that Satan was a beloved angel who became jealous and disrespected God, and that is how the war began and has been leading mankind astray ever since. So Lord, it seems to me that all the trouble started in heaven. How can God blame man for bringing the world to ruin by sinning when it's really heaven' fault for letting Satan come down here and roam around earth like he owns it?"*

Jesus said, *"My child, mankind's troubles did not start in heaven, and there is not one inch of Earth that Satan owns. Everything on earth belongs to heaven; nothing belongs to Satan. The problems caused by Satan began within his own heart. He refused to listen to God, and he chose to break away from God's heavenly family and set himself apart. As I told you, Satan would be forgiven if he could find it in his heart to apologize to God. But to this day, Satan has not found the courage, or the sincerity, to say he is sorry and seek God's forgiveness. Satan will not apologize.*

Think of the families you knew while you were growing up. In some families there is often a child who, no matter how hard the parents beg for him to be good, he refuses and shuts himself off from the love his parents offer him. That is how it is with Satan. He turned away from God's freely offered love, like a petulant child who runs away from a loving home. God has remained with his obedient and loving children in heaven, and all who love and obey Him are welcome there.

But all that happened in heaven, between Satan and God, happened before God made the planet and before the creation of man. When God created man, Satan has been trying to trick humanity with lies and temptation, hoping that man will love the sin of the devil, more than the goodness of God. Satan hates suffering in isolation and, rather than be alone, tries to lead as many souls as he can away from the light of God's love and into wickedness and evil. Satan wants man to suffer with him, to be cursed as he is cursed, for there is no suffering greater than to live without God's love. Satan knows how much God loves mankind, and that gives him even more pleasure when he corrupts a human soul. He wants God to suffer.

Remember this my child, God's love and light are the only safeguard against evil and eternal darkness. Tell all those who will listen to prepare their hearts for the Day of Judgment, for the last days of Earth draw near. Satan is the author of all lies and is not to be trusted. He has been trying to separate mankind from God's love since Adam and Eve."

I then asked, *"That reminds me, Lord. I know a student can sometimes be a greater tutor than his teacher, and in the same way, a beginner can become a much greater sinner than those who committed the original sin. But I have a question about the original sinners, Adam and Eve. They are the ones who started all this trouble. Why did you create them in the first place? If they had not eaten the forbidden fruit, the rest of us would still be living in paradise. There are many more sinners in the world today than back then, but we all came from Adam and Eve, so all mankind must have learned to sin from Adam and Eve, right? You are the Almighty, so you must have known when you created them that they were weak and they would sin sooner or later. You can't deny that, Jesus! So why did you do it? Why create two sinners who will end up bringing suffering and misery to every human who was born after them? Honestly, I think it was a mistake. You should not have created them.*

Jesus said, ***"When you have a child, you do so out of love. You do not know if that child will be good or bad, but you love that child with all your heart and you hope for the best. You hope the child who is given life by God will continue to think of God."***

I have another question, *"There is something else I don't understand, how do you want us to think of God? You have said that I should think of God as my Father, that God the Father loves me even more than my parents, that God knew me in the womb and loved me before I was born. But I have only just met you, Jesus. I have only been introduced to God in the past weeks. However, I have known my parents since the day I was born. Ever since I was a child, I saw my parents struggling to do their best for me and laboring to keep me fed and sheltered. So do you really expect me to love God more than my parents, who have always given me everything I have ever needed since I was born."*

Jesus said, ***"So, you want to distinguish the love of your parents from the love of God?"***

I said, *"Yes, and I think I have a good reason to distinguish between the love of my parents and the love of God. I have always seen my parents show their love for me. They have always protected me and taken care of me. But I never saw God love me when I was a child. I never saw Him working in our bean field to provide for our family, put food on our table, or make clothes to keep us warm."*

Jesus said, ***"My child, even if you never saw Me, I was always there watching over you. Have you heard the song, 'My Protector Who Loves Me.' I gave you your parents to protect you for Me."***

I told Him how grateful I was for answering my questions.

But I still had more questions, *"So, should I call my parents a gift or a grace?"*

Jesus said, ***"They are not grace. They are my gifts to you, because they were My apostles when they had you."***

I said, *"But I have heard about 12 apostles. Do you mean I come from them? Were they the parents who gave birth to everyone in the world?"*

Jesus said, ***"There are two different types of apostles, those who are chosen for the hands-on***

work, and others who were chosen to spread my words.

I said, *"So, you mean the apostles are many but only 12 are well known since they are apostles of your words?"*

Jesus said, ***"Yes."***

I asked Him again, *"People don't seem to understand what is happening in Kibeho. They are complaining. Why don't you give them light to see as they have many doubts?"*

Then Jesus said, ***"Those who don't believe in Kibeho, tell them to believe and follow what is in the Bible with all their hearts."***

Then I asked Him *"But the Bible has many different translations by different religions. They changed some things. How will we know which one to follow? Also, I see that those you have appeared to are Catholics. What are we supposed to understand from that, that we should maybe follow only the Catholic Bible?"*

Then Jesus said, *"The ones who believe in Me and follow My commandments, no matter where they are I will find them. When I come, I will not come looking into the Catholic Church to see who is a good Christian. There are many people in different religions who are good people, who do good deeds of love, and who honor my commandments. The difference is that they each follow the culture of their religion, but on the other hand they should love sincerely. In whatever you do, do it with faith and love."*

I said, *"Thank you so much for answering my questions. May everyone have faith in You. May the whole world love You and know who You are."*

When Jesus spoke to me about the end times and the end of the world, I was scared. So I asked Him more questions. *"I have another ques-*

tion, how will you protect people who work for you, in the last days? What if they fall in the trap of the devil in the last days and yet have worked for you all their lives? And what will happen to those who don't do good and maybe in the last days they might recognize the devil? It wouldn't be fair to those who have worked for you all the time. In the last days, it might be confusing for many people to recognize the work of the devil. I have many more questions actually. Today is a day of questions."

Jesus said, *"I am Almighty. I will look into people's hearts. If I see someone who falls into the devil's war and yet was a believer, I will save them."*

I said, *"What about the ones who have done wrong and who will recognize the devil's war?"*

Jesus said, *"Those kinds of people would have worked for the last days, not for heaven."*

I asked Him, *"But you told me that at the end, purgatory, the place where people go to purify themselves before going to heaven, will not exist. So, where will those people go who have sinned most, but who have recognized the devil's war? Will they go to heaven without going to purgatory to purify themselves even if they haven't worked for you all their lives?*

Jesus said, **"Do you understand what I am trying to tell you?"**

I said, *"No."*

Jesus said, **"I mean, it would be too late for such a person. Working for the last day will not mean they had changed their hearts."**

I told Him I had another question, *"You know, when I think about everything, there are many of us who love you, who put our trust in you. In those last days with all the temptations, what kind of grace will you give us, to resist the devil, to endure* those hard times? I am asking you, please don't keep it from me. You are sending me, and you know it is not easy to be a messenger."

Jesus said, *"I will give a sign to those who believe in Me, a sign from heaven."*

I was very thankful and said to Him, *"Thank you very much, I pray that people will continue to believe. I pray that many will change their hearts and believe in you. I will tell them to respect you and honor you always. I will tell the whole world so they will know who you are. I will even tell my friends, and not only friends my age, but also those who are not my age. I will tell everyone I meet."*

PRAYER JOURNAL

PRAYER JOURNAL

REGARDING INDIVIDUAL DEATH

Jesus told me, *"Go and tell people to do penance from now on. There is not much time left before Satan comes to tempt you. Let each of you seek out My truth, and follow the path I have laid out in the Bible for all mankind to follow. Let each man and woman be faithful to every word that I have spoken. Let all who are aware that I walked on this earth before, be aware I will hold each of you accountable and judge if you have lived your lives according to My words, for My words are heavenly treasure. All who seek earthly pleasures above the truth of My words are risking their eternal souls. Read the words that have been recorded in the Bible, for you may be certain that all I say is true and will surely come to pass. The entire project that I have planned will be realized."*

He also said, *"The last day will come and it will consist of two levels: For each person, the last day is the day of his death, and for humanity, it is the day of my second coming."*

He also said, *"The last day is near, however the most important day is the individual death, which may come before the very last day, because the one who dies with sins will resurrect with sins, and the one who dies with holiness will resurrect with holiness. The last day of the world, will not change the outcome of a personal death."*

This is how Jesus said we should prepare for our individual death, because it is more important to think of and prepare for this day than the end of the world.

I. First, we must know the commandments of God and we must follow them. We must leave the bad behavior of this world behind and practice the virtues that lead us to heaven.

II. Second, we must be prepared at all times, because we do not know when our own death will come and we must keep it in the forefront of our minds. The time will take us by surprise.

III. Third, we must learn to pray. Prayers are not only words. When we pray, our prayers should also show in our actions. We should practice good behavior, loving actions and help our brothers and sisters.

IV. Fourth, we must confess our sins regularly, and become newly created, like we were at the time of our baptism.

PRAYER JOURNAL

PRAYER JOURNAL

ABOUT THE END OF THE WORLD

Regarding the end of the world, Jesus said, *"The world will end…not because people are bad, but because God created it knowing that one day it would end. However the troubles and hardships that will happen in these times will be brought about by people themselves because of those who have refused to repent of their sins."*

Jesus continued, *"The one who confesses their sins with true sorrow, I forgive them. The one who doesn't repent of their sins, I remain angry with them because of their sins. That is why, before I return to earth again I will bring back my anger that I kept for those who have refused to repent. Then I will give my anger to my seven angels who will spread it to all the four corners of the world. After they have spread it, all kinds of troubles will start to emerge from all over. Everything will continue to deteriorate. However, remember that it will happen because of those who would have refused to repent of their sins."*

PRAYER JOURNAL

PRAYER JOURNAL

BEFORE JESUS RETURNS, SATAN WILL COME TO TEMPT PEOPLE

———

Jesus said, *"Before the end of the world, Satan will do all things possible to tempt the world. He will tempt people in many ways, especially by material goods earned without working for them. The enemy will intensify his strength in the very last days."*

Jesus also said, *"Those forthcoming times, those times that are leading up to God will be times of trials, times when each person will have to bear his own cross. The one who would follow Me will have to suffer. Any person who would take the road to heaven will walk in suffering, until the day when he will find eternal rest. From that day on, he will suffer no more. However the one who takes the road to Hell will walk with no difficulties, yet in the end he will suffer, and his suffering will last forever."*

He then said, *"Do not be afraid, but have faith! For the one who does good will come with me to Heaven. It is the one who does evil who will be burned by fire. Therefore, hurry to do good, for Satan will one day disappear from this world, and then you will never be tempted again. But hurry, for there is little time left."*

He also said, *"Anyone who will come calling himself Jesus, don't believe in him. The one who will come saying that God and Satan are brothers, don't believe in him. Anyone who will come saying that Jesus sent him to give you a message and you must go through him (this person) so he can show you how to reach God, don't believe him. The one who will lead you on the bad road, you will know him right away. The one who leads with truth, you will know him as well."*

Jesus continued, *"The ways in which Satan will try to deceive in those days will be many. For example, he might come and stand where you can hear him well. He will say that he is Jesus and is coming to heal people. He will be singing how he can't find anyone to heal anymore. So people will run to him so he doesn't leave.*

Jesus said, *"He will trick people. He will show them miracles and tell people that he will heal them and so they will come to get healed. He will say things like, 'If I go, don't say I didn't try and tell you."*

Jesus added, *"Other things Satan might use to attract people will include bringing food and telling people that he is doing what Jesus did in the past, feeding the hungry. The food will have poisons that will blind people's hearts from the truth and the love of God and neighbor. Satan will do many things. For example, a bad rain might come and people might not be able to go to work. Then he will come afterwards and say how he saved you from the rain and now he is coming to give you food, though you would not have worked for it. And you might think he was so kind and then accept the bad food he is offering you. Don't accept it."*

Jesus said, *"Don't accept his lies or his food. It will not be the first or last time people will not have everything they want, or will lack food for a night or two, but rather, know that I am with you and pray to Me to sustain you in a true way. He will not come giving food. When He comes, and passes by the blind, the blind will retrieve their sight. The deaf will hear. The sick will be healed just from Jesus passing by. Jesus Christ will not come drawing attention to Himself."*

Jesus said, *"People must return to loving one another and they must turn back to God. Satan will come calling himself Jesus and other names, and sometimes he will call himself a messenger of Jesus who is coming to do all the miracles Jesus did in the past. Satan will be coming seeking attention and calling himself the Son of God. He will want you to see the good he has done. He will say, 'You see I saved you from rain, you see, you see...' and so on. I will not come in this manner feeding people."*

Jesus added, *"When I come, I will come like a traveler, but if I walk past a deaf man, he will hear. If I walk past a blind man, he will open his eyes and see. If I walk past a mother, she will be full of joy. The one who loves me, even if he is un-*

der a bridge, I will find him. Let it not be said that one must live on the top of a mountain, or perhaps God will not find them. Even if you are under a hill, I will still find you. Know that this is not your home, your home is not this world, but heaven is your home."

PRAYER JOURNAL

PRAYER JOURNAL

HOW WE WILL KNOW WE ARE LIVING
IN THE END TIMES

Jesus said: *"In the last days, the sun will be very hot and many people will die from famine and other calamities that will follow this famine. There will be many temptations from the devil in those times, because there will be greater suffering on earth than the world has ever known before."*

Jesus continued, *"People on earth hardly listen. They follow the one who misleads them and don't follow the One who leads them in truth. I see that many don't believe in Me. They don't believe in My work. Yet, tomorrow they will believe in the work of Satan. Satan doesn't want you to be happy. He is like a child cursed by his parents, who wants to make sure that he is not alone to suffer. He wants everyone to be cursed with him and he will do anything to attract them. This is the nature of Satan."*

Jesus then said *"You will know that My return is near when you see the explosion of wars between religions. When you see that, know that I am on the way back. Once the wars of religions begin, nothing will stop the fighting. Towards the end, there will be wars, and nation will fight against nation, and religion will fight against religion. Families will also fight against one another. Parents will fight their children and children their parents and children will fight among themselves. Many miseries will follow because many people will continue to refuse to repent."*

At hearing all that, I was scared and I asked Jesus, *"Why will the religions fight when they are all working for you?"*

Jesus said, **"Religions will fight among them-selves because they lack enough love. They say that they love Me, but in reality they don't love Me enough. They say that they are working for Me, but truly, many don't work for Me the way I want them to. The lack of love between religions is what will cause wars among them."**

Then I asked Him, *"How will fighting among children and parents happen when you know the love between a parent and a child?"*

Jesus replied, **"To start fighting, people will have had enough of the world and the world will have had enough of people. That's why I am here to tell you that I am on the way back to earth. I warn** *you! Be patient with all that will tempt you. Those who will believe in Me, they will be persecuted heavily. I am telling you don't be discouraged, I will be near you. When all the bad things will be happening and have made you exhausted, the sterile will wish to be a tree, and a mother will wish to be sterile in vain. Man will wish to die in vain. There will be many earthquakes in all the corners of the globe. In many places, the sun will beat down so relentlessly that the earth will dry up and crops will fail year after year. Winds will carry away all the soil, and never-ending rains will bring great flooding. Hunger will grip many nations. Many will fight each other for food, and scores will starve to death."*

I asked Him again, *"Knowing that things will be like that, why did you create man with weakness, and yet you knew well, man wouldn't survive such temptations?"*

Jesus said, *"Man is always with weakness, but he doesn't have to remain so. I came Myself on earth to be his example. I was born as flesh and blood to be a living example for mankind of what ways are possible for humanity. I showed mankind the path to follow in life and I showed him the way to heaven. I came in the nature of man. I showed you how to suffer the pains of the world and how to love God and I showed you His love. I came Myself to save you, because I saw that you had difficulties in trying to live a pure and godly life. I descended from Heaven to heal the sins of the world."*

Jesus continued, *"Man saw what I had to endure because of his sins. I was stripped naked, beaten and crucified and mankind bore witness to this. I died for man's salvation. My goal was to show you that all those who want to follow Me will be persecuted. But tell them not to deny Me because I will be beside them always."*

Then Jesus told me, *"I gave man the example when I told my Father that His will be done, not mine. I wanted to show you that your will is not the most necessary to be done, but My will has to be done in you."*

Jesus continued, *"I gave man an example until my last breath on the cross where I said Seven Words for man to remember."*

These are explanations Jesus gave me:

I. He prayed for those who killed Him. *"Forgive them Father, for they know not what they do."* He prayed, because He wanted to show us that He is going to heaven without anger towards those who killed Him. He also wanted to teach us that He was here to open the Kingdom of Heaven for us and that before His death no one had reached heaven. He wanted to show us that from now on, we are

His brothers and sisters and children of His Father. Before He died we were servants in this world.

II. Jesus healed a thief on the cross. *"I tell you the truth, today you will be with with Me in paradise."* He wanted to show us that He is salvation for everybody. He wanted us to know that He loves sinners who repent and leave their sins; it is for this reason, Jesus descended from heaven to earth. He didn't come for the righteous. He came for sinners. However, Jesus hates sin. That is why He is close to the sinner, not to the sin.

III. Jesus confided His Mother to us. He gave us a Mother when He called John and said, *"Here is your Mother."* and then said to His Mother, *"Woman, here is your son."* The Virgin Mary is the most loved by the Father and the most loved by the Holy Trinity. That is why Jesus asked her to inherit all the children of God - so she can take care of them in prayer. Jesus also wanted people to respect Her, and to know that they have a Mother. He wanted to teach us that His Mother would be praying for us, even praying for those who ignore Her Motherhood.

IV. He asked His Father, *"Why have you forsaken me?"* He wanted to show us that every human being can be weak, but doesn't have to remain in weakness.

V. He told His Father, *"I am thirsty."* He wanted to show us that we must be thirsty for the things of heaven. Having that thirst is to thirst for the love of God in our heart - this is the love that stays with us all our life. Anyone who loves God must be thirsty for Him, and must hunger to remain in His love.

VI. He told His Father, *"It is accomplished."* Jesus was happy that He accomplished the work His Father had given Him, a mission accomplished without losing any of the people His Father entrusted to Him. He was also happy to be an example of showing love to all those who had done wrong to Him. He wanted to show us that in order to follow God, we must make an effort to do good, especially to those who perpetrate wrongs against us.

VII. He told His Father, *"Into your hands, I commit my spirit."* He wanted to show all who want to follow God that they should put themselves into His hands – complete surrender. They should entrust all their affairs into God's hands because He is the true shepherd, without whom, we can accomplish nothing.

Jesus then said, *"I became your example, but the troubles will only increase because of the sins of those who refuse to repent. Know that nothing shall stop those troubles because of the hard-hearted."*

Jesus added, *"Even those who are mine and are doing things right, will be persecuted and will have to endure this suffering as well. But be patient with all that will tempt you. Don't deny Me; I will be near you."*

He also said, *"Because of those who have refused to acknowledge and repent of their sins, difficulties will increase. Demons will come from all corners of the world and will start to tempt people with all sorts of miracles telling you that, 'I am Jesus. I am here to end all your problems. I will give you everything you want and give you all you are lacking."*

Jesus said, *"Don't accept these demonic lies."*

After hearing those words, I was scared and asked Jesus, *"Why will those demons come to us, and how can we protect ourselves from them? How will we recognize them, and not confuse them with you?"*

Jesus answered me, ***"When you hear someone claiming to be Me, or acting in My name, but use words that contradict those I have said in the bible, you will know they are demons trying to lead you away from the Light of God. Don't accept them."***

I said. *"How are we going to get out of that?"*

Jesus replied, ***"Prayer and enough love for God. Many times people ask themselves what is the right attitude to take so that God can approve their prayers? In principle, prayer doesn't have limits. You are addressing yourself to God wherever you are, whoever you are and whatever the state of your soul. Ask and then thank God, whether you*** *receive or not. What matters most is that you trust in God. On the cross, I prayed for everyone and I became your example."*

I said. *"What will become of sinners if there is no priest for confession?"*

Jesus said, *"After all, it is not the priest who heals the sins. The priest receives the sins, and presents them to Me. I heal them. He helps Me to save the world. To all Christians, when you confess your sins to God, and regret them from your heart with sincerity, you too are helping Me to save the world, because you hate that which I hate - the sin. When you tell the priest the sins you have done, it is God you are telling about them. The priest is not replacing Me, because I live always."*

I continued. *"Some people are saying that if God was truly Our Loving Father, He would never allow an innocent child to die. Or, if God was really good, why would He create Satan? Why would He permit so much death, destruction and suffering?"*

Then Jesus said, **"God doesn't want to destroy men. He displaces them and calls them to Himself so that they can share His happiness. This is what men must know."**

I asked Him again, **"So what do you want me to share with the world?"**

Jesus then said, **"The message I give you to share with the world is not a new message, it is the same words I spoke when I was on earth. Most have forgotten these words. They put them aside as if they don't concern their lives; they forget that I am their Shepherd. All of My words contain your salvation. That is why I want you to go and remind people of this wisdom I shared with the world before when I was on earth."**

PRAYER JOURNAL

PRAYER JOURNAL

WOE TO THOSE WHO WILL BE PREGNANT AND
BREASTFEEDING WHEN JESUS RETURNS

———

He continued to tell me, *"Because of those who have refused to repent, there will be many trials, but woe especially to those two groups of people when I return. Those who will be pregnant and those who will be breastfeeding during those times."*

I replied, *"You tell me that for people who are pregnant and breastfeeding, that those days will not be easy for them? Why? We have the same body and suffer the same way; it will not be fair to them. I would assume they would be protected more since they are with child?"*

Jesus clarified, ***"I am speaking about those who are pregnant with sins, who have sinful plans, or who are breastfeeding others by leading them to sin. Of course, pregnant and breastfeeding women will suffer more, because they will be carrying another person; it is the same as those who are breastfeeding their babies. But those who will suffer without measure are those, men or women, who will be pregnant with sin or breastfeeding sin in others."***

Examples of those who are "pregnant with sin"; those who are doing wrong and hide their sin include:

I. A person who has killed another and then runs through the village asking, "Who is it that killed that person?"

II. A prostitute who has just done her act of prostitution, and runs to laugh at her sisters practicing the same prostitution, asking, "Who can do such a thing?"

III. A thief who steals his brother's belongings and runs to ask, "Who stole those things?" when he knows fully what happened.

IV. A person who causes conflicts between people and goes to ask, "Who did it?" Knowing wholeheartedly what they did.

Examples of those who "breastfeed others into sin"; those who do wrong in the eyes of their brothers and sisters, and encourage others to follow their example are:

I.   A prostitute who incites others to perform the same acts.

II.   A thief who calls his friends to go and steal with him.

III.   A liar who incites his brothers and sisters to lie.

IV.   A killer who asks his friends to kill.

V.   Any person who does wrong and incites others to do the same by convincing them or showing them a bad example. That person, no matter what gender they are, they are spreading or 'breastfeeding' sin.

Jesus continued, *"I have the capacity to look into the hearts of people; I can see the heart of a person that is like a spoiled smelling fruit because of their sins."*

Then Jesus said, *"It is those that I refer to as being pregnant with sins or those who are breast-*

feeding sins. Those who are in trouble are those who will be carrying those sins at the time of my return. They are in trouble because they will not see Me and will not reach the Kingdom of My Father. They are in trouble because without repenting they will burn in the eternal fire that was created for Satan and his bad angels."

PRAYER JOURNAL

PRAYER JOURNAL

HIS RETURN—THE LAST DAY AND DAY OF JUDGMENT

Jesus then said, *"Before I come back on earth, everyone will suspect it. My return will look like a tree that is about to dry out. My return will show the same signs of the changing tree. Everyone can see that change is coming and something different is about to happen."*

He said further, *"Before I come back, I will put love into My people, so they will know it is Me who is about to come back, and no one else. On the last day, the earth will tremble, and joy will be overwhelming. I will send My angels from the four corners of the sky, from the East to the West, from the North to the South. The angels will assemble all people, they will put the good on one side, and the bad on the other side. The rainbow will traverse the sky in that instant, to show you the promise I made to the world. Then you will see Me coming, carrying my glorious cross that I saved you with, emerging from the brightest cloud. There will be many angels all around Me, and then I will come as the just judge. At the sight of My cross that I will be carrying, everyone will tremble, good and bad, and the dead will be resurrected. Then I will judge everyone. Nothing will be hard anymore. I will show everyone how they have worked, and each will decide himself the place where he deserves to be. Nobody will be able to repent anymore, it will be too late. This will confirm what is said by the apostles, that you are not of this world, and the world doesn't belong to you. Then you will leave earth without taking anything, either to go to heaven if you are good or to go to hell if you were bad. You will understand that each soul belongs to God and it doesn't die like the body. Rather, the soul will be punished if it has done bad in leading the body astray. That is the eternal death that will never be forgiven or changed."*

He continued and said, *"Everything you see here on earth will burn and end, but the promises I made with the world will remain. To start, the sun and the moon will fall on earth, then fire will come from inside the earth and burn everything that remains on earth.*

He then said, *"I will judge the bad first and tell them, 'You have refused to do what I asked you to do, like Satan who refused to do My will, go to his side and burn along with him. Then I will turn to the good, and tell them, 'You have done My will, come with Me so that I can give you the reward of your life in my Father's house where you will be happy eternally."*

After Jesus spoke these words, He said to me, *"Go and hurry to do good; do all I have asked you to do. The one who knows a little will be asked a little; those who know a lot, will be asked a lot. I don't mean that those who want to know more should stop seeking, but let them continue striving to know more and those who are doing good works, let them continue to do more good."*

I then asked Jesus, *"When people die, many go to purgatory. On the last day, will we all go through purgatory with our bodies?"*

Jesus replied, *"Purgatory will not exist anymore. People will have suffered enough in the world in the last days; their purgatory will have finished. The good will go to heaven and the bad to hell."*

I asked, *"Why don't you tell people what day the end of the world will be, so they can convert? If you did, they would all do so."*

Jesus said, **"I don't know the day of the end of the world, but if people knew, they would convert out of fear, not out of love. In the Kingdom of God, there will only be those who have been convert-ed by love because of immense love that has been shown to them on the cross."**

Jesus then said, **"I don't know the day nor do the angels know the day, only God the Father knows the day. You don't have to be preoccupied by that day, because when an individual dies, that is their last day. There is an individual last day, and a collective last day. Nothing will stop the last day from coming. It was always in God's plan to prove His Power, to manifest His Love to the world** *and to let them know that they don't belong to this world. The last day for everyone is very near, but the most important one is the individual last day, because the one who will die with sins, will resurrect with sins, and the one that will die without sins will resurrect without sins."*

PRAYER JOURNAL

PRAYER JOURNAL

WHAT IS THE TRUE RELIGION?

———

I asked Jesus, *"On earth we have many religions, which one is the true religion?"*

He told me, ***"There are many religions on earth, but it is not Me who created them. They were created by people who separated themselves. I have founded one religion and that is the religion of love. A religion that baptizes in the name of the Father and of the Son and of the Holy Spirit, a religion that follows My commandments, is a religion that saves."***

PRAYER JOURNAL

PRAYER JOURNAL

WHAT JESUS SAID ABOUT THE RICH
AND THE POOR

Jesus said, *"There are two things which you see on earth, but the way you see them is different from the way I see them: the rich and the poor. The poor to Me, are the ones who love Me, and the rich are the ones who don't love Me, and their earthly wealth is useless in that way. If you possess much, but you love Me and you are doing My will, and you respect all My commandments, I see you as poor; I consider the poor the ones who do My will."*

He also added, *"If you don't have anything to eat and drink, or to wear and yet you do not do My will, and you don't respect My commandments, I see you as a rich man. But also, if you are poor, and don't have anything to eat or to wear, and you are doing My will, and respecting My commandments, I see you as poor. If you are rich and have all the wealth in the world, but you don't follow My will and don't respect my commandments, you are rich to Me. And if you are rich and have all the wealth of the world, and yet you are doing my will, and you are respecting My commandments, you are poor to me."*

He added, *"The rich man to Me is the one who refuses to do My will. It does not matter how much or how little one has. Those who do My will, respect My commandments, they are considered poor to Me. Those who don't, no matter how much* or how little they have, they are considered rich to Me.

He said again, *"Woe be to the rich in their hearts. If they don't convert and change their hearts, they will not come to live with Me in the eternal happiness in heaven. If they don't change, they will burn forever in hell that was created only for the devil and all that belong to him. I have told them to follow my will and they chose hell."*

He continued, *"Blessed are the poor at heart, because they are doing My will. And everything they want of Me, they will see it. The poor at heart want to heal from sin, and I will heal them. The poor want eternal rest, I have it and I will give it to them. They want to reach eternal happiness and joy in my Fathers' house, I will give it to them."*

PRAYER JOURNAL

PRAYER JOURNAL

ABOUT MARY

A man who was not catholic asked me, *"For us, our religion tells us that we don't have to consider the Virgin Mary in a special way. They tell us that she is a woman like any other, but Catholicism says that if you don't say the rosary, you will not go to heaven. Mary is very important to you. For us, she is a woman like another. What does Jesus say about that?"*

I told him, *"Nobody says that those who don't say the rosary will not go to heaven, but what Jesus said about the different religions was that those who know more will be asked more. You will be judged from what you know. What you don't know, you will not be asked. I will not ask you to be Catholic because I know or think that I know better. Rather, I will ask you to continue to believe sincerely what your religion teaches you if your religion teaches you to love in the ways of God. Follow the commandments your religion gives you, and nothing will stop you from going to heaven. You must follow the promises you made to that religion."*

I added, *"If you are Catholic, and you know the importance of Mary and you don't respect her, you will be asked about that."* Being a young man I asked him, *"Truly think of what you know of your mother, from the perspective of our culture, the value we give to our mothers. Do you want your friends to respect your mother? What place do you give her in your life, among others?"*

The boy said, *"Well, I love my mother, and, of course, I will do anything for her and I don't want anyone to disrespect her. She is a special woman."*

Then I said, *"So, you think Jesus is not smart or good enough to appreciate His mother? The Holy Trinity chose Our Lady to be the mother of Jesus. God sent His angel to deliver a message to this chosen woman, and The Holy Spirit chose to come to her to bring Jesus into her womb. Jesus respects His mother who raised Him, and so we too honor her and He wants us to respect her as well."*

"How can man love someone and yet, at the same time, despise the person's mother? How can we love and adore Jesus and at the same time cast His Mother aside? The Blessed Mother is the Mother of the Whole World, she is the Mother of all creatures and even those who don't know her, they are still her

children. She helps them to pray to God, even without them being aware. She is the mother of all men. This is because God Himself has wished it thus. How dare we say that she is or was, just an ordinary woman, no different from any other? God is warning us to-day of this grave disrespect, so that we may be able to change.

PRAYER JOURNAL

PRAYER JOURNAL

GOD IN THREE

One time I asked Jesus, *"I hear people say that there is three Gods and yet there is ONE God. What does it mean and how should I respond to those who don't understand?"*

Jesus said, *"Yes they are right, there are three Gods, but they are ONE God, because ONE combines the other two. There is God the Father, God the Son and God the Holy Spirit. God the Father combines the Son and the Holy Spirit. God the*

Son combines man. He is God/man who came to save people. God the Holy Spirit is God that lives in each man to give him strength to work and to purify himself."

PRAYER JOURNAL

PRAYER JOURNAL

BAPTISM IN THREE WAYS

Jesus continued, *"I want to tell you about the three ways of baptism: <u>baptism of desire</u>, <u>baptism of blood</u> and <u>baptism of water</u>. Baptism of water is when you get baptized by the water in the name of the Holy Trinity and one God. The baptism of blood is given to a person who dies defending faith. The baptism of desire is given to the one who did loving deeds and dies without getting a chance to be exposed to the baptism of water. If, for example,* *they lived in a place where faith in God was not introduced yet."*

Jesus continued, *"No one will receive three baptisms. You can only receive one. When I come back on earth and I find somebody who has one of those baptisms, who has done My will, I will take them to have their eternal rewards in heaven."*

PRAYER JOURNAL

PRAYER JOURNAL

IN SPEAKING ABOUT THE YOUTH

———

Jesus said, *"You the young. It is you who will work for Me tomorrow. You are the hope of the world. How will you work for Me if you don't change your heart and decide to do good? How will you work for Me if you don't let go of the bad behaviors of all sorts? How can you work for Me if you don't let go of the sins of theft and fornications? How will you work for Me if you don't do My will?"*

Jesus continued to talk about the youth. *"You, the youth, if you don't change your hearts and your behavior, you will not see Me and you will not reach heaven. Rather you will suffer eternal torment in hell forever with the devil and all that belongs to him if you refuse to repent."*

PRAYER JOURNAL

PRAYER JOURNAL

WHAT JESUS SAID ABOUT MARRIAGE

Jesus said, *"When a man has two wives, they are killers of My commandments. The second wife is an adulterer like all adulterers because she is committing adultery with the man who has the sacrament of marriage with the first wife. The second wife is a murderer like any other murderer, because she is killing the love and the peace of the first wife, who has the sacrament of marriage, because she stole her husband."*

He continued, *"The second wife is a thief like any other thief because she is stealing the husband of the wife who has a sacrament of marriage. The second wife is killing my commandments. My ninth commandment said that you shall not wish for another's blessings, another wife's husband or another's marriage that is not yours."*

Jesus continued, *"A man who has two wives is like the second wife. He is a killer like any other killer, because he is killing the promises he made to his first wife and to Me and to others. A man who has two wives is a thief like any other thief. He is stealing from God, who gave him permission to have one wife, yet he gave himself two wives."*

He continued, *"A man who has two wives is killing my commandments. My ninth commandment said that you shall not wish for another's blessings, for a woman that is not yours."*

PRAYER JOURNAL

PRAYER JOURNAL

About riches:

Jesus said, *"Man is foolish, he runs after worldly things yet knowing full well that a day will come when he will have to relinquish these. He is chasing the wind. Some people do not believe in the existence of Heaven. They say that the only Heaven is on this earth. Yet on this earth, all are poor. All need the gifts of God. Poverty is not a lack of money nor is it a lack of food to eat. The only real poverty is the lack of grace that leads to the Lord. The possessions of this world are only ashes, while the only true riches are the riches of the heart."*

About religions:

Regarding the great number of churches that all claim the same founder, Jesus, He said, *"God is like a Father who has many children, but they should take care not to divide themselves. They should rather try to receive the word of their Father in the same way. God wants all of us to be united, for all of us to pray with one heart, to have the same faith, to all serve the same one, true God. There is no other way that leads to God. I have only one religion, a religion of love and people should think of that always."*

Regarding His passion:

Jesus told me, *"We must do penance every Friday, the day on which I suffered death for you, in order to help in the salvation of souls."*

About Heaven:

Jesus told me, *"Some people say that they will attain heaven through bribes in a similar manner to the bribery that seems to pay off for them on earth. Regarding this belief, it must be emphasized that the only gift that man can offer God is a true prayer from the heart."*

Regarding the prayer of the rosary:

Jesus stated, *"The rosary of Our Lady is the true strength of a Christian who prays it. Nothing is better able to convert a Christian than a Rosary that is prayed from the heart, while meditating on its virtues and endeavoring to put them into practice in one's life."*

About prayer:

Jesus said, *"Let men pray with fervor, all together, with one heart, with one voice. Let them stop asking for miracles. For they live with miracles, and it is not miracles that will get them to heaven. Let them rather pray to Jesus, and pray to the Blessed Mother, with a prayer that comes only from the heart, not just from their lips. In our prayer, we should always thirst for God."*

ABOUT SEGATASHYA

Among the many prophesies Jesus gave to Segatashya, one of the most significant for him personally, was that he was going to come to heaven before he reached Jesus' age. Everyone knew of this prediction and people waited to see when he would die. Sadly he died when he was only 28 years old. He was killed in the Genocide just as Jesus had prophesied.

PRAYER JOURNAL

ABOUT THE AUTHOR

Immaculee has written a number of books, the most widely read being *"Left To Tell"* and its sequel, *"Led By Faith"*. In *"Left to Tell"* Immaculee details how she survived the genocide in her homeland Rwanda in 1994; hiding in a tiny bathroom, three feet by four feet, with other seven women for an unbelievable ninety-one days. *"Led By Faith"* describes the next 10 years of her life, recovering from the loss of most her family and the more than one million of her fellow countrymen. She tells us it was a terrible time for her but one that taught her many lessons about life. Among them she learned how vital love is, and how damaging lack of love can be. She explains how necessary forgiveness is to our good health, both of body and soul, and how possible it is to forgive even when we think it is impossible. During those unspeakable, horrific times, Immaculee's faith was also renewed, and it is the most important thing in her life today. This is the reason why she has continued to write about her experiences. She writes about her faith with messages that encourage others to grow in their faith. Immaculee has since written "*Our Lady of Kibeho*", "*The Rosary: The Prayer that Saved My Life*" and "*The Boy Who Met Jesus*" all of which contain the tools that helped her remain close to God in those trying times, and kept her safe.